Contents

What to Do 2

An Elephant Calf 4

Becoming an Orphan 6

A Park for Orphans...................................... 8

Caring for the Orphans 10

Dika – An Orphan Elephant Calf............ 12

Back to the Wild... 14

Something to Think About 16

Do You Need to Find an Answer? 18

Do You Want to Find Out More? 19

Word Help 20

Location Help... 23

Index 24

What to Do

Choose a face

Remember the colour you have chosen.

When you see your face on the page, you are the LEADER.

The LEADER reads the text in the speech bubbles.

There are extra words and questions to help you on the teacher's whiteboard. The LEADER reads these aloud.

When you see this stop sign, the LEADER reads it aloud.

STOP
My predictions were right/wrong because . . .

You might need:

- to look at the WORD HELP on pages 20–22;
- to look at the LOCATION HELP on page 23;
- an atlas.

If you are the **LEADER**, follow these steps:

1 PREDICT

Think about what is on the page.

- Say to your group:

"I am looking at this page and I think it is going to be about . . ."

- Tell your group:

"Read the page to yourselves."

2 CLARIFY

Talk about words and their meaning.

- Say to your group:

"Are there any words you don't know?"

"Is there anything else on the page you didn't understand?"

- Talk about the words and their meanings with your group.
- Read the whiteboard.

- Ask your group to find the LET'S CHECK word in the WORD HELP on pages 20–22. Ask them to read the meaning of the word aloud.

3 ASK QUESTIONS

Talk about how to find out more.

- Say to your group:

"Who has a question about what we have read?"

- Question starters are: how..., why..., when..., where..., what..., who...
- Read the question on the whiteboard and talk about it with your group.

4 SUMMARISE

Think about who and what the story was mainly about.

When you get to pages 16–17, you can talk to a partner or write and draw on your own.

An Elephant Calf

I am looking at this page and I think it is going to be about… because…

When an elephant **calf** is born, it stands quickly on its feet. A young elephant drinks milk from its mother for a few years.

An elephant calf learns many things from its mother. It learns how to use its **trunk**.

The mother elephant is very **important** to an elephant calf.

Are there any words you don't know?

Who has a question about what we have read?

Let's check: important

Why do you think the elephant calf stands quickly after it is born?

Becoming an Orphan

I am looking at this page and I think it is going to be about… because…

Elephants travel a lot. Sometimes they have to cross rivers. A calf can be washed down a river. Or it can fall into a hole. When a calf is **separated** from its mother, it becomes an **orphan**.

Sometimes a calf becomes an orphan because its mother has been killed.

Are there any words you don't know?

Let's check:
separated

Who has a question about what we have read?

Why do you think a mother elephant might have been killed?

A Park for Orphans

In the wild, an elephant calf needs its mother. It can't live without her. It can become ill.

Some people, called **keepers**, take care of the orphan elephants in a park. The keepers take care of the elephants until they can take care of themselves.

Then, the keepers take the elephants back to the **wild**.

I am looking at this page and I think it is going to be about… because…

Are there any words you don't know?

Who has a question about what we have read?

Let's check:
wild

Why do you think an elephant calf could become ill without its mother?

Caring for the Orphans

The keepers teach an elephant calf how to drink. They put the **tip** of its trunk on a **blanket**. A blanket feels like its mother.

In the wild, an elephant calf will go under its mother to get out of the sun. At the park, the keepers put an **umbrella** over them.

I am looking at this page and I think it is going to be about… because…

Are there any words you don't know?

Let's check:
tip

Who has a question about what we have read?

Why do you think the blanket feels like its mother?

The keepers are teaching a calf to drink.

This page was mainly about fact fact

STOP
My predictions were right/wrong because . . .

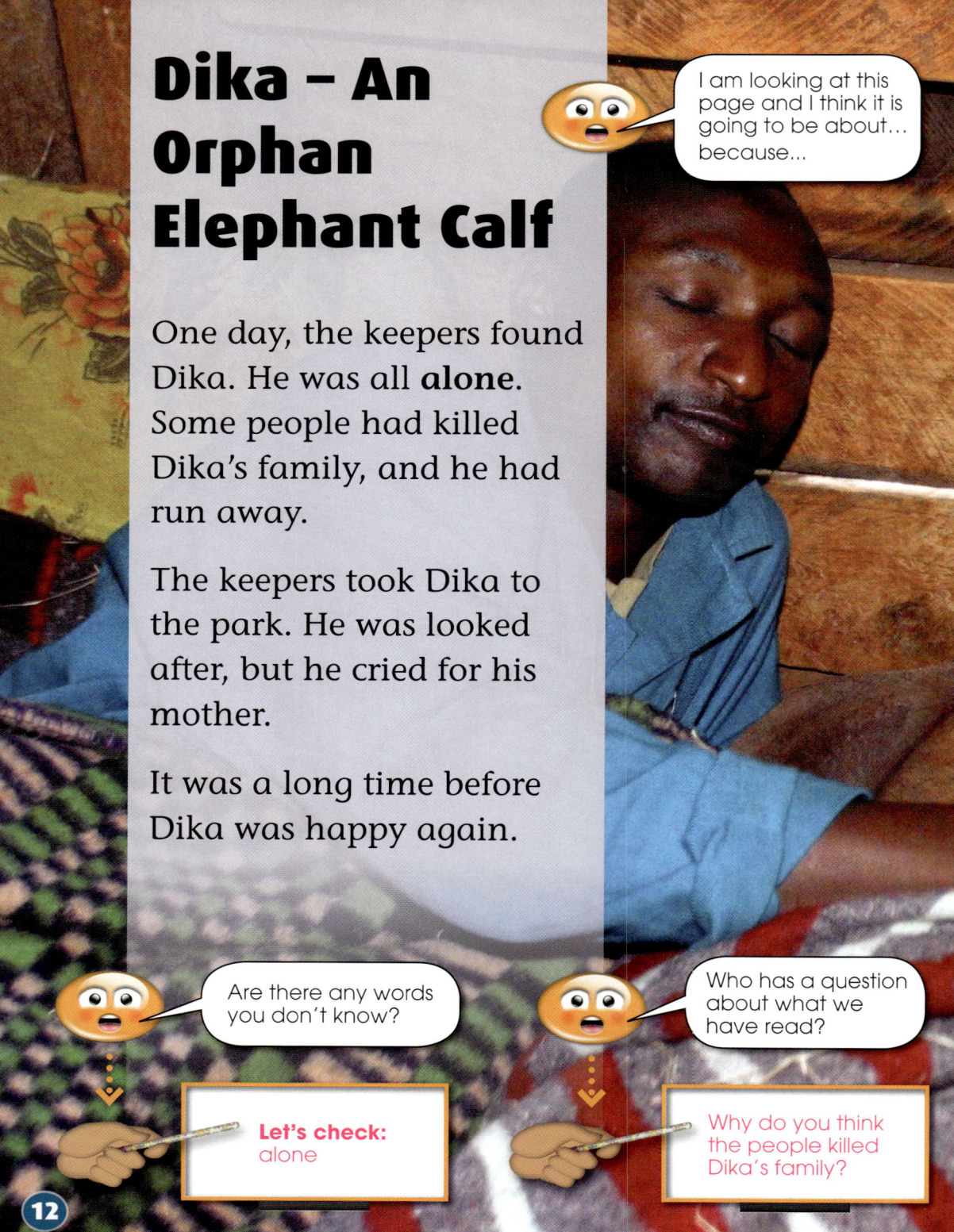

Dika – An Orphan Elephant Calf

One day, the keepers found Dika. He was all **alone**. Some people had killed Dika's family, and he had run away.

The keepers took Dika to the park. He was looked after, but he cried for his mother.

It was a long time before Dika was happy again.

I am looking at this page and I think it is going to be about… because…

Are there any words you don't know?

Let's check:
alone

Who has a question about what we have read?

Why do you think the people killed Dika's family?

Back to the Wild

I am looking at this page and I think it is going to be about... because...

Dika was ten years old before he could live in the **wild** again.

Many years later, he came back to the park. He had some **wire** around his leg. He needed the keepers to help him.

Orphan elephants don't forget where they were cared for.

Are there any words you don't know?

Who has a question about what we have read?

Let's check: wire

Why do you think elephants don't forget where they were cared for?

Something to Think About

 or

Think of some important facts and some interesting facts about orphan elephants. Talk about your ideas with a partner, or write them down.

Important Facts

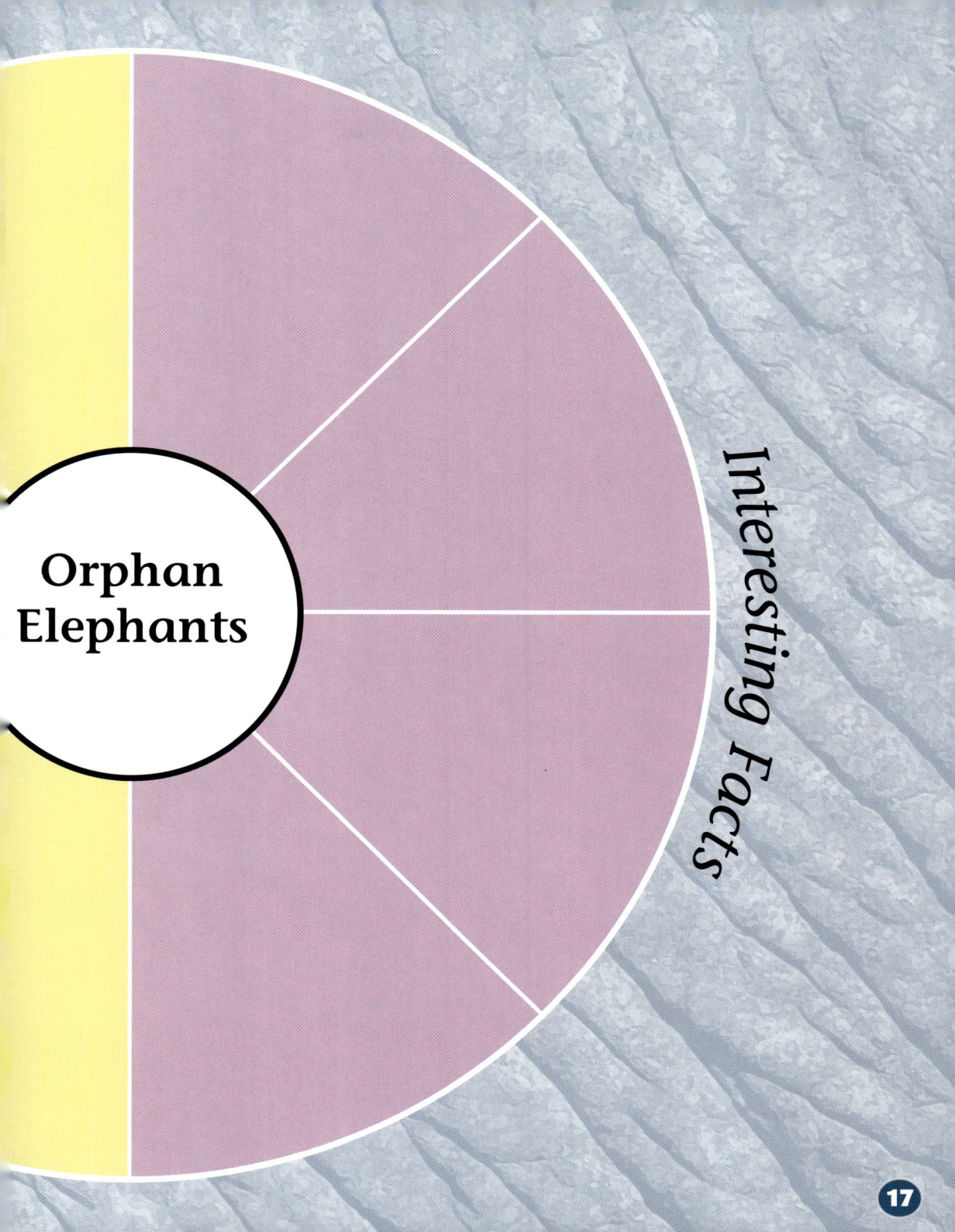

Orphan Elephants

Interesting Facts

Do You Need to Find an Answer?

You could go to . . .

Library >

Expert >

Internet >

Do You Want to Find Out More?

You could look in books or on the internet. These key words could help you:

animal orphans

animals in the wild

animal park keepers

Dika, elephant orphan

elephant calves

elephant parks

Word Help

Dictionary

alone	not with others
blanket	a cover that is usually used on a bed
calf	a young cow, elephant, seal or whale
important	needed
keepers	people who take care of animals in a park or a zoo
orphan	a child or a baby animal without a mother or father
separated	to be apart from someone or something

tip	the part right at the end of something
trunk	the long nose of an elephant
umbrella	a tool that keeps off the sun or rain
wild	a place where animals live free
wire	a long, thin strip of metal that can be bent into different shapes

Word Help

Thesaurus

cross	go over, through
happy	glad, cheerful, pleased
teach	train, show
tip	end, point

Location Help

The Elephant Orphan Park is in Kenya

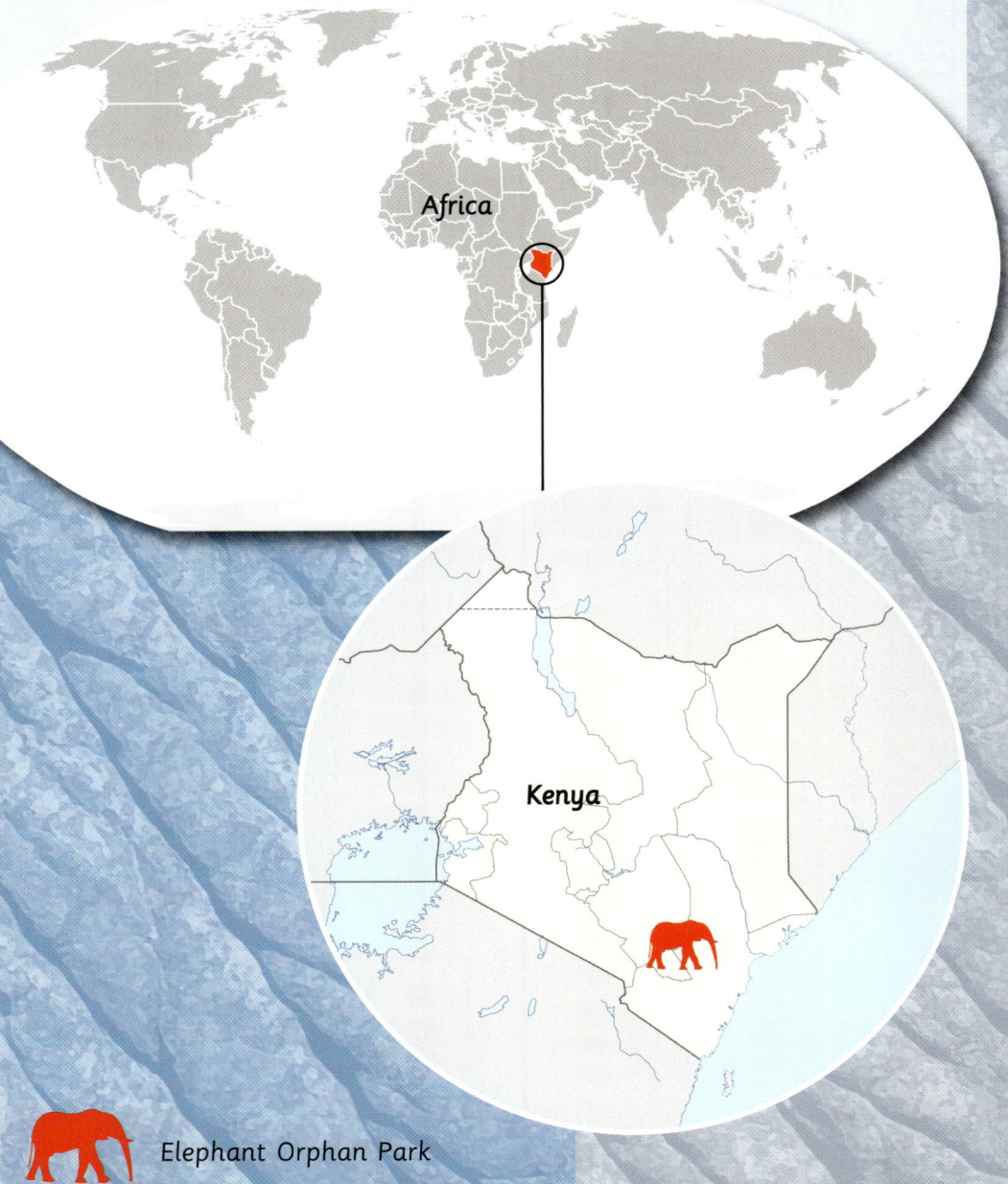

Elephant Orphan Park

Index

Dika 12–13, 14–15

family 12

keepers 8–9, 10–11, 12–13, 14–15

mother............................... 4–5, 6, 8, 10, 12–13

orphan 4, 6, 8–9, 10, 12–13, 14

park 8–9, 10, 12, 14

wild...8, 10, 14